A near contemporary of Mickey Mouse, Hector Breeze has been little influenced by the work of William Hogarth (1697-1764). When not reading the paper, thinking or looking for cardboard he lives quietly at the edge of a field.

Also published in this series:

The 100 best jokes of **MICHAEL HEATH**

Watch out for further volumes!

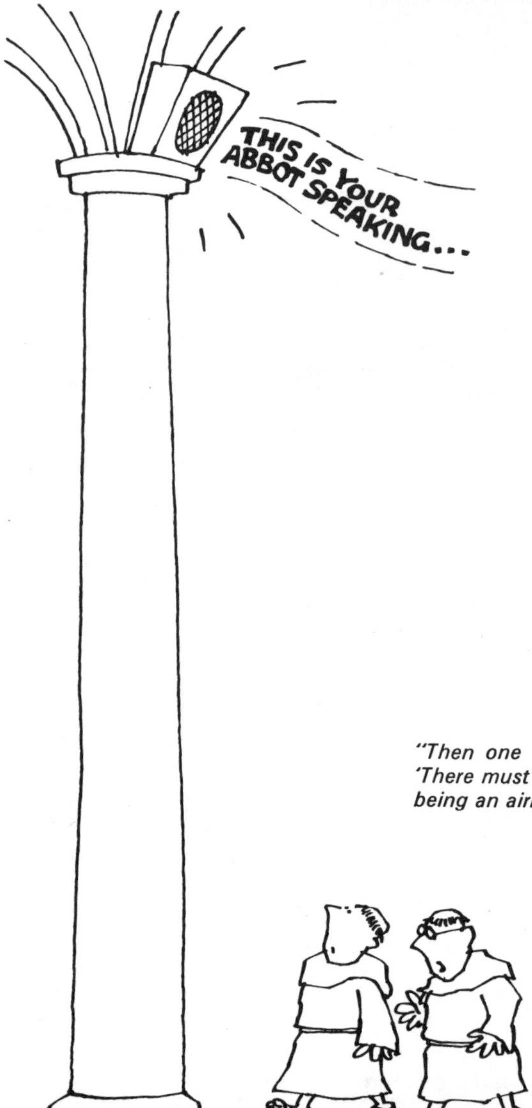

"Then one day he thought: 'There must be more to life than being an airline pilot . . .' "

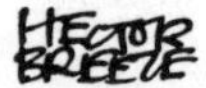

Private Eye Cartoon Library 2

100
best jokes of

A Private Eye Book
with Andre Deutsch·London

Published in Great Britain in 1973 by
Private Eye Productions Limited,
34 Greek Street, London W1 in association
with André Deutsch Limited,
105 Great Russell Street, London WC1.

SBN 233 96448 7

Some of the following cartoons were drawn for this book. Most were first seen in Private Eye. *Others appear by kind permission of the* Evening Standard.

Made and printed photolitho in Great Britain by
Ebenezer Baylis and Son Limited
The Trinity Press, Worcester, and London

"I thought my first-class honours degree in English Literature would at least have got me into the Obscene Publications Squad"

HECTOR
BREEZE

"My client does not intend to remain a peeping tom, m'lud – he hopes to become a top international espionage agent"

"Do you have to spend your days off whistling solemn music?"

"All right, you own the means of production and distribution. Now what?"

"You're lucky, Mrs Prindleby – most shoplifters aren't rich enoug to be kleptomaniacs"

B. THRIBTON
GENEALOGIST
—
YOUR
ANCESTORS
TRACED
HECTOR
BREEZE

"Am I glad to be home! It was packed solid all the way from Waterloo!"

"What do you mean 'It seems like yesterday'? It was *yesterday!"*

"I'm Inspector Grimfold of Plain Clothes and I'm taking you in for impersonating a police officer"

"All right, I'll go over the strategy just once more: Get in There and Smash His Face to a Pulp'"

"All right, so you're an atheist! So you're going to be re-cycled!"

"It's my considered professional opinion, Mrs Stapley, that you need to go on a long sea voyage . . ."

"I don't know whether it's environmental pollution, but there are fewer four-leaf clovers nowadays"

"Well, I like to hear it occasionally!"

"They might put one up to you – you're unknown"

"You know as well as I do, Hilda – I haven't got enough in the Post Office to make my break with the Establishment"

"I wonder if you could possibly direct me to the Old Kent Road"

"They never cater for those of us who see all the issues in varying shades of grey"

"Thank you, Carbloe – that's enough participation for today"

HECTOR
BREEZE

"You know the rule, Gilcroft, about getting ordained during office hours"

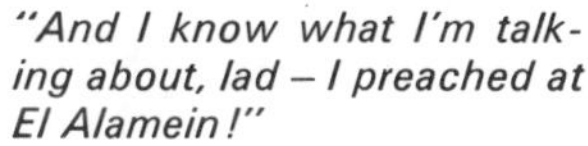

"And I know what I'm talking about, lad – I preached at El Alamein!"

CRABTON'S
ICES

"He says he's not retiring until somebody's stopped him and bought one"

"He's not only a born actor, he was conceived on the stage"

"When your name's restored to the register! I don't believe it was ever on *the register!"*

THE JUNIOR BUS CONDUCTOR

"You realise of course that they're attempting to condition you into early acceptance of the work principle?"

"You could have made something of your life, Mibson. You could have become an officer *of the cloth!"*

"That's all I ever hear: 'just one more sitting'!"

"I mean, what's it going to look like in my obituary notices?"

"What's the matter – didn't you like *being evacuated?"*

"I take it all rooms are equipped with water-beds?"

$XY = \frac{a^3}{b} + x\frac{(n-1)}{2y}(a+b)^4 + n(b-4)($

$= HCO_3 \rightarrow 4CO_2 = \int_0^a \frac{dy}{dx}[m+n^2]$

$= \sin\frac{\pi}{4} \log nx + e = \Delta ab\ (8$

$= \sum AB + \tan M\theta \operatorname{cosec} 4° = 9$

$x = \frac{(100-t)a - 100b}{b} = \sqrt{4}$

$\operatorname{cosec}\theta - \tan A = 4(a+b)^2$

$= \frac{x^4 - y^4}{a^2b^2c^2} = \log ex + 7{\cdot}834$

$= \cot an\ \theta + \sqrt[3]{b^2 - 4ac} + \frac{}{a}$

$= \frac{n-4}{n} + 6x + y^2 + a^2b^2 + c^2 =$

"There's more to it than just getting to the bottom right-hand corner, Wiblington"

"Your humans are undone"

"It is my duty to inform you that while under surveillance you have been observed to smile at thirteen other dogs"

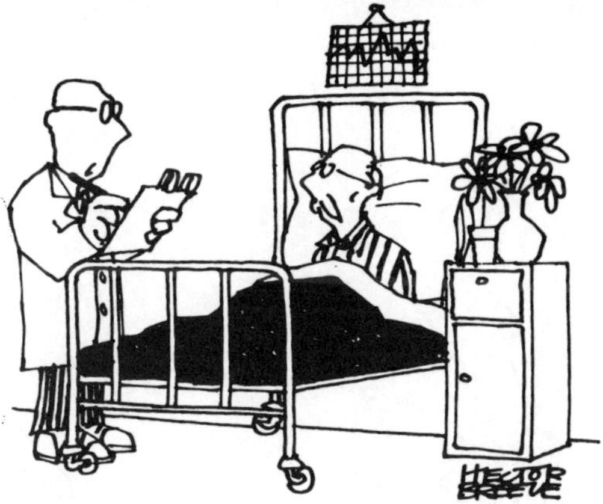

"There's nothing to worry about. Undergoing terminal experience isn't as bad as it sounds"

"Before we converted this place it used to be a tram"

"Who wants silver spoons these days? I was born with a high credit rating!"

"How do they expect you to work off your aggressive tendencies with that?"

"Well, I don't feel inhibited by the fact that it's a cliche situation"

"Let's play tycoons and secretaries. How's your shorthand?"

YOUR NOTE'S ON THE TABLE
HECTOR BREEZE

"There must be some rational explanation"

PERSONNEL
MANAGER
HECTOR
BREEZE

"You and your Drive-In Doss Houses Ltd!"

"You're suffering from paranoia. Any-one'll tell you"

"Human chauvinist"

"Well, we can't have a holiday there again – you've been sentenced to death in your absence"

"According to our tax advisers we need a salesman with a lack-lustre approach"

SALES
PERSONNEL MANAGER
HECTOR BREEZE

"How does the Fire Service strike you?"

"And my dad's more of a reactionary, bourgeois, consumer society-orientated, hypocritical, time-serving old bigot than your dad!"

"Conchie!"

"I hate to think what it would be like if I hadn't been to Business School"

"This is one of those occasions when I say to myself 'what does it all mean?' "

"First day at grammar school and he's a Pillar of the Establishment!"

HECTOR BREEZE

"I've never seen you flick an imaginary speck of dust off your cuff"

HECTOR
BREEZE

"Don't forget – I fought at El Alamein so you could be free to worry about the collapse of the eco-system!"

"An eight million pound grant and we could breed the whitest elephant the world has ever seen!"

HECTOR
BREEZE

". . . If you ask me sir that last goal was a fluke . . . of course we were very lucky with the weather . . . ah no the way I go I take the A23 as far as Crawley . . . load of rubbish sir I switched off after the first ten minutes . . ."

"He describes himself as a compulsory ownership transference executive, m'lud"

"When you said you lived off the land I thought you meant you were a property speculator"

"And ignore any whispers you may hear about favouritism, Dad"

HECTOR
BREEZE

"Frederick Arthur Criblington, 37, a scrap dealer of no fixed address – this is Ronald Arthur Bimley, 24, unemployed of Leytonstone"

"This surely *must be the thick end of the wedge"*

"Yes, I have *tried the Executive's Register!"*

"I'm beginning to wish I'd never heard of the Ronald Thurcroft Memorial Trust!"

"No, it doesn't bring back memories – it's a 1962 remake"

"Oh, go on, Miss Herbcroft – you say that to all your secretaries"

"It says: 'You have been specially selected by computer not to receive our pornographic advertising material"

"This is what I like – the hiatus between the post mortems on last year's Christmas broadcast and the frantic search to find a theme for this year's"

"And he was just learning to laugh at misfortune, doctor, when he dislocated his jaw"

"Off to join a commune for the middle-aged petit-bourgeoisie, that's where!"

"I've never liked to ask him why he was reduced to the ranks"

ANTI-
DEODORANT
HECTOR
BREEZE

"Ah well, back to the sandwich board"

"You've got the support of the moderates . . ."

"It says: 'Do not break the chain. When your name reaches the top of the list you will receive a rates demand, an electricity bill, a telephone account, an income tax assessment and a notice of foreclosure' "

"It's a repeat of a temporary fault first shown on BBC-2"

"I had hoped that Mr Chamberlain would be on at eleven o'clock every Sunday *morning"*

"Permission to go beserk, sir!"

"My agrophobia's coming on again"

"Why do we pay seven pounds a year to watch all this gratuitous violence?"

"Damn good chap that Barber . . .

About time we all stood on our own two feet . . .

No, no, old boy – it's all on Amalgamated Durables Ltd."

"We'd all like to be strip club proprietors, Milcroft"

"There's your trouble, lady – it's full of instant mashed potato"

"Don't tell me – it's another programme about the Second World War"

"Looking on the bright side, Arthur meets a nicer type of person at the Labour Exchange these days"

"I don't know about you, but I'm pinning all my hopes on being a late developer!"

"Move about a bit! Anyone can see you're the store detective!"

"By the time I was his age I was reading balance sheets"

"What's all this 'For God's sake stop reading that blasted paper. Edith' mean, Edith?"

"So he's studying English Literature! So he can write my company reports!"

"Or, if you were a conscientious objector, a fortnight in the prison of your choice"

"How do you expect to get anywhere if you're itinerant?"

"Have you any pornography suitable for an elderly maiden aunt?"

"I like your qualifications, Gribson – you have the makings of a first-class underling"

"The trouble with Eric is he can't bear to throw anything away"